Leadership Reading

Spilling the Tea On How Top Leaders Read

Avil M. Beckford

The Invisible Mentor Press

Contents

Chapter 1

Introduction

My Story

On October 3, 2012, I got a call no daughter wanted to receive. My mother died unexpectedly from a heart attack. My heart shattered into many pieces. To work through my grief, I did something I love --- reading. I created a challenge for myself to read the world. At the end of the challenge, I visited over 30 countries via the books I read.

Reading the world was a transformative experience. However, one thing I noticed when I was reading nonfiction books along my journey, I kept on experiencing déjà vu. Haven't I read this before, haven't I read this before? It was very frustrating, so I set out to find a solution. I conducted research to find a solution because I thought there had to be a better way to read nonfiction.

I learned traditional publishers had word counts. And so, to satisfy the word counts, authors often added extra information. How many case studies or examples do you need to understand a concept?

While taking the PhotoReading course offered by Learning Strategies, I learned that only four to 11 percent of the text on a page of a nonfiction book carries meaning, according to Russell Stauffer. You read that correctly. It's not a typo. That's about one sentence. Most of the information adds context to that one sentence. The results reminded me of Pareto's Principle, also known as the 80/20 Rule.

This made me realize that the 80/20 Rule also applies to reading, so you can read 20 percent of the book and understand 80 percent of the text. But the trick is to know which 20 percent to read. And this information is part of what I reveal in Leadership Reading: Spilling the Tea on How Top Leaders Read.

After I completed the Read the World Challenge, I created for myself in 2013, I developed reading programs that others could take part in. Since then, these programs have grown into what they are today. Through my research, I have been able to offer leadership development programs that allow senior level leaders to shave hours off their reading time when digesting a book.

My Journey to Leadership Reading

Luminaries read a lot of books. But contrary to what you see and read in the media, most of them are not reading a book cover-to-cover. When these accomplished individuals take up a nonfiction book, they intend to read it with purpose. They usually struggle to solve a problem or have questions they want the book to answer. When they read, they read the chapters and sections of the book that have the information they need. When they read, they are looking for specific pieces of information.

For years, I have been calling this type of reading selective reading and strategic reading. However, in 2021, after reading *Turn the Page* by Chris Brady, I learned about "leadership reading." Leaders read to learn what they need to know. The concept was what I was calling selective reading.

When people learn about leadership reading, they immediately think it's skimming and scanning. But it is not even close to any of those two forms of reading. Yes, the leader is not reading the book cover-to-cover, but he or she reads deeply the sections of the book that apply to him or her. That's a huge difference.

Definition of Leadership Reading

"Leadership reading is reading with a bent toward making the page impact our lives. It is more than just pleasure, although it can be immensely enjoyable. It is more than reading a lot of books, although it will certainly take us through many volumes. Leadership reading is the active, intentional devouring of the greatest writings applied with earnestness toward the highest aspirations. It is a lifestyle habit that is open to everyone but taken advantage of by only a select few." Source: Turn The Page by Chris Brady.

What the definition of leadership reading tells me is that leaders read with purpose. And that is something I teach in the leadership development courses I teach. A leadership reader reads more books since the focus is on problem-solving and answering questions. And they get more from their reading time because they are so focused.

Leadership reading refers to the act of reading with a specific purpose. The goal is to gain knowledge, skills, and understanding that can apply to the role of a leader. It involves reading books, articles, and other written materials that help them improve their abilities and decision-making processes.

Importance of Reading for Leaders

The importance of reading for leaders cannot be overstated. As leaders, it's important to stay informed and up-to-date on the latest ideas and trends in your field of work and industry. Reading allows leaders to expand their knowledge base and develop a deeper understanding of their profession and the challenges they may face as leaders.

Reading more books enables leadership readers to get more ideas. And to the outside world, they appear to have the Midas touch. However, it's not just about new ideas found on the pages of a book. It's also about new ways of looking at the world. And the new perspectives they bring to old problems.

Most professionals want to become a leader. And they often think that reading leadership books will help them become better leaders. And yes, the information in the best books can help them achieve that goal. However, leadership reading is not about reading leadership books.

The important thing to note, though, is that leadership reading is not just for leaders. Anyone can practice this type of reading if they understand what it entails. And when you get to the heart of things, anyone can become a leader. Even if it is leading yourself. Leadership reading helps you to become a more effective leader.

Impact of Leadership Reading

The impact of leadership reading can be significant. It has the potential to improve decision-making skills, enhance communication abilities, and increase overall knowledge and understanding of industry trends. Reading helps leaders think critically and analyze information, which can be valuable in solving problems and making informed decisions.

Reasons Leaders Should Read

There are several reasons leaders should make reading a priority. Reading helps leaders stay current and informed about trends and developments. Reading also helps leaders develop new ideas and approaches to leadership, which can be invaluable in today's rapidly changing business world.

Besides staying informed and developing new ideas, reading helps leaders improve their communication skills. By reading a wide range of materials, leaders expand their vocabulary and improve their ability to articulate their thoughts and ideas clearly and effectively. This is beneficial in both written and verbal communication. And helps leaders better communicate with their team members, colleagues, clients, and other stakeholders.

Studies show a correlation between vocabulary and income. With different experiences and perspectives, leaders develop a better understanding and empathy for others. This helps build effective teams.

Outcome of Reading Leadership Reading: Spilling the Tea on How Top Leaders Read

After reading Leadership Reading: Spilling the Tea on How Top Leaders Read, you will become a leadership reader. And you will never approach reading the same way again. You will get tips on how to read books to solve the problems you have and answer questions. It will also help you learn how to select books that apply to your interests and goals, how to read them effectively, and how to apply what you learn.

However, I will take things further by teaching you how to use leadership reading to be seen as an authority and build your personal brand. To use the knowledge in books to build thought leadership requires that you engage in network note-taking. You will learn how to connect the information from the books you read. This allows you to see what others miss. The most successful people know how to do this. But they will not tell you because it is a part of their leadership and competitive edge.

Chapter 2

PART ONE:
THE ABCS
OF LEADERSHIP
READING

P art One of Leadership Reading: Spilling the Tea on How Top Leaders Read is a guide to mastering the art of leadership reading. This section is divided into five chapters, each focusing specifically on the steps necessary to become a successful leadership reader.

The first chapter, "Prepare Your Mind," provides readers with the tools they need to prepare their minds before reading a nonfiction book. This includes writing a one-sentence purpose for reading the book, creating questions you want the book to answer, and performing exercises, so the reader is in a relaxed yet alert state, so she uses both sides of the brain.

The second chapter, "Preview the Book," will teach readers how to preview a book to determine which sections to read. This involves understanding the structure of a book, identifying the key themes and topics, and evaluating the relevance of each chapter to your reading goals.

In the third chapter, "Read," readers will learn how to read only the sections and chapters they flagged as important during the preview stage.

In the fourth chapter, "Take Notes" covers note-taking techniques and strategies for remembering information.

Finally, in the fifth chapter, "Become a Leadership Reader," the author pulls everything together to show readers how they can become a leadership reader. This includes strategies for applying what they've learned in their lives and achieving their leadership goals through reading.

Overall, Part One of "Leadership Reading" provides readers with a framework for becoming a successful leadership reader. From preparing their minds to reading strategically, readers will learn how to maximize their reading time and gain valuable insights that help them in their professional and personal lives.

Chapter 3

Prepare Your Mind Before Reading a Nonfiction Book to Remember More of What You Read

To fully absorb and remember the information presented in a nonfiction book, it's important to prepare your mind first. By taking the time to prepare your mind before reading, you increase your focus, comprehension, and retention of the information.

Many people read nonfiction books because they struggle to solve a problem. Or they have questions they want answered. Having a purpose for reading, crafting questions you want the book to answer are part of the leadership reading process, but not the only one.

And performing exercises that connect both sides of the brain, so you're feeling relaxed yet alert, is also important. Doing this gets you into the ideal state for learning. I've included several exercises, so choose a couple. Not all the exercises will resonate with you.

Setting Intentions

Writing your one-sentence purpose and crafting questions you want the nonfiction book to answer before reading is a powerful tool for improving focus and comprehension. This helps to direct your attention to engaging with the material.

Be specific: Identify a specific outcome you want to achieve through your reading. For example, instead of saying "I want to learn something new," try saying "I'm reading [name of book] by [name of author] because I want to develop my critical thinking skills."

Write it down: Write your intention before you read. This helps to make it more concrete and reminds you of your goal as you read.

By setting a specific intention before reading, you focus your mind and increase your motivation to engage with the material.

Brain Gym Exercises

Brain gym exercises are a set of simple exercises designed to stimulate and activate both sides of the brain. These exercises help to improve focus, concentration, and overall cognitive function. By connecting both sides of the brain, brain gym exercises, you improve the ability to process and remember information.

Some examples of brain gym exercises include:

Eye movements: These exercises involve moving the eyes in different directions, such as up, down, left, and right. These exercises stimulate the visual processing centers of the brain and improve focus.

Crossing the midline: This exercise involves crossing the body's midline with different movements, such as reaching across the body with the opposite arm or leg. This improves communication between the left and right sides of the brain.

Writing with the opposite hand: This exercise requires writing or drawing with the non-dominant hand. It stimulates the brain and increases creativity.

Brain Buttons: This exercise involves using the fingers to press on specific points on the face, such as the temples or the bridge of the nose. This stimulates the brain and increases focus.

The Energizer: Stand with feet hip-width apart, arms at your sides. Inhale and sweep your arms overhead, then exhale and bring them back down to your sides.

The Hook-Up: Sit with your feet flat on the floor, hands on your knees. With your eyes closed, imagine a line running from the center of your forehead, through the crown of your head, down your spine and out through your tailbone.

The Elephant: Standing with your feet together, raise your arms above your head and then bring them down to your sides, mimicking the trunk of an elephant.

Jumping Jacks: More than likely you've done jumping jacks before, even if it was when you were a kid.

These are just a few examples of brain gym exercises you can do before reading nonfiction to help prepare the mind.

Alpha Brainwave State

The alpha brainwave state is a relaxed yet alert state that occurs when the brain is producing alpha waves. This state is characterized by a lower frequency of brain waves, typically between 7 and 14 Hz. When the brain is in this state, it is more relaxed and less reactive to outside things. This makes it easier for the brain to focus on what it is doing.

Research has shown that when you are in an alpha brainwave state, it is easier to read. This means that you can focus on what you are reading. To achieve an alpha brainwave state, it is important to relax the body and minimize distractions. Some tips for achieving an alpha brainwave state before reading include:

- Finding a quiet and comfortable place to read where you will not be disturbed

- Relaxing your body by taking a few deep breaths, stretching or meditating for a few minutes before reading

- Minimizing distractions by turning off your phone or closing unnecessary tabs on your computer

- Listening to calming music or nature sounds, which can help to relax the mind and reduce stress

- Incorporating alpha brainwave-inducing techniques such as binaural beats audio, guided meditation or progressive muscle relaxation to help achieve the alpha state

Binaural Beats Audio

Binaural beats are an auditory illusion that occurs when two different sounds of similar frequencies are played simultaneously, one in each ear. The brain then perceives a third sound, known as a binaural beat, that is the difference between the two frequencies.

Binaural beats audio can help prepare the mind for reading by altering the brainwaves to specific frequency ranges. The most common frequency range for reading is alpha brainwave state (7-14 Hz) which is associated with relaxation and focus. Binaural beats audio in the alpha frequency range helps to improve focus and concentration. This makes it easier to process and remember the information you read.

Some specific binaural beats audio recommendations for reading are:

- **Alpha Wave**: Binaural beats set at 7-14 Hz, which helps to improve focus, concentration, and overall cognitive function.

- **Focus and Concentration**: Binaural beats set at 14-16 Hz, which helps to improve mental clarity, increase focus and concentration.

- **Study Aid**: Binaural beats set at 18-22 Hz, which helps to improve memory, learning ability and focus.

It's important to note that everyone's brain waves respond differently to binaural beats. Try different frequencies and find what works best for you. Use headphones while listening to binaural beats audio, because it's how the binaural effect is produced.

Lazy 8

Think of the number eight (8) lying on its side. This exercise connects both sides of your brain.

- Extend your arms in front of you, clasp your hands together with interlocked fingers and your thumbs pointing up towards the ceiling. Move your arms first to the top left and continue in a sideways figure "8" motion. Come upwards through the middle of the "8".

- As your arms move through the figure "8", your eyes should follow your thumbs through the motion. Be sure to move only your eyes and not your head as you do this exercise.

Three Fingers Technique

The three fingers technique is a simple yet effective method for focusing the mind before reading. I learned this technique in the Silva Method Basic course. It involves using the index and middle fingers pressed gently against the thumb. You tell yourself you're going to remember the information, and you have superior concentration, making it easier to process and remember the information you read.

Here is a step-by-step guide for performing the three finger technique:

- Start by sitting in a comfortable position with your back straight and your feet flat on the ground.

- Close your eyes and take a few deep breaths to relax your body and clear your mind.

- Place the tip of your index and middle fingers on the top of your thumb.

- Press gently on each of the areas with your fingers. And tell yourself you'll remember the information. Say the name of the book and the author's name.

- When you are finished, take a deep breath and open your eyes. You should feel more alert, focused, and ready to read.

It is also good to combine this technique with other brain gym exercises, binaural beats, and alpha brainwave state for optimal results.

Chapter 4

Preview the Nonfiction Book Before You Read to Find the Sections That Apply to You

P reviewing nonfiction books is a great way to gain a better understanding of the book before reading it. It allows you to get a summary of the book's content and decide if it's worth your time. Previewing also helps you differentiate between books on similar topics and decide which one is most beneficial for you.

Having a clear understanding of what the book contains helps you determine if the book's purpose aligns with your own needs and interests. Previewing nonfiction books helps you become more familiar with the author's writing style, voice, and tone. This is extremely helpful when deciding if the book will be an enjoyable read.

Reading an entire book only to find out it's not what you're looking for wastes your time. That's why previewing a nonfiction book before diving into it is incredibly beneficial.

Steps to Preview a Nonfiction Book

Read a Good Summary of the Book

Reading a good summary of a book is helpful because it gives you a helicopter view of what the book is about. When you read the book, you'll have a place to hang the information. Many websites provide summaries of books, as do newspapers and magazines. You can also find many of these summaries available for free online.

I would be remiss if I didn't mention that I have a membership site, the Art of Learning Leadership Academy, where you get access to Bookish Notes. My Bookish Notes are more than book summaries and will help you develop expertise and thought leadership.

Read the Preface

Reading the preface of a book gives you insight into its author's purpose and the story of why it was written. It's an essential part of understanding the text and provides a valuable context for the rest of the work. Taking the time to read the preface helps you better comprehend the entire book. It's also a great way to gain an understanding of the author's perspective and style of writing.

Reading the preface helps you determine if the book is a good fit for you. And if it contains content that applies to your interests. By reading the preface, you can decide if this is a book you would like to read further and gain more knowledge from. Taking the time to read a book's preface gives you a better appreciation for the work and helps you become a more informed reader.

Read the Foreword

Reading the foreword is a great way to get a better understanding of a book's content and its author's message. It summarizes the content and allows you to make an informed decision on whether the book is worth your time and attention. A foreword is a short review of a book, usually written by someone other than the author. The person may be a friend, family member, or a colleague.

The person who writes the foreword discusses the author's personal background, any interesting stories they have shared, or even how they came to write the book. The foreword offers an insight into how the book was written, and any difficulties the author faced writing the book. By reading the foreword, you will understand the author's purpose in writing the book and get a better idea of the themes and topics covered throughout.

Read the Introduction

Reading an introduction is a great way to gain insight into a new topic. It's important to read and understand the introduction before diving into the content. Introductions are typically concise and summarize the topic, allowing you to get a sense of what the book is about and what to expect. You'll also find the primary and secondary ideas here.

They often provide definitions of key terms, summaries of important points from the main body of text. And an outline of the argument or structure of the text. Once you have read the introduction, you can use it as a foundation for understanding the material. It helps you identify relevant passages in the text as you read.

Understanding the introduction to any new piece of content makes it easier for you to understand and refer to when needed. I've also found that sometimes the introduction is so detailed that you don't need to read the book. It goes back to your purpose for reading the book.

Flip through the Book

Flipping through the book's pages gives you an overview of the topics it covers. This helps you get an idea of its level of complexity and how it may be beneficial to you. You'll also see the images and charts included in the book.

View the Table of Contents

Reading a book is a great way to spend your free time. But it's important to make sure you're picking the right book. That's why it's so important to view the table of contents of the book before you read. Doing this gives you a clear idea of what topics the book covers and its structure and organization.

This helps you decide if the book is right for you. When you have a good idea of what to expect from the book, you can more easily determine how long it will take you to finish it.

The table of contents helps you decide which chapters and sections align with your purpose and answer the questions you crafted. Take a few moments to examine the table of contents and make sure you're getting exactly what you want out of the book.

Before you move forward in the leadership reading process, make sure you understand the table of contents. Think of the table of contents as a skeleton that holds the book together. What do you already know about the topic? Jot down the information. Check the index to see if the items on your list are there. This helps you to qualify the author. Is she or he an expert?

View the index

The index is an organized list of all the topics and subtopics the book covers. It's a helpful tool for both understanding the content and for navigating quickly to the sections that interest you. It's a great way to get an overview of what you'll be reading and to find out what specific topics are discussed.

Looking at the index gives insight into the book's organization and structure. This helps you get the most out of your reading experience. If you're knowledgeable about the topic, when you view the index, if certain information is missing, it's a red flag. And an opportunity to question the expertise of the author. So view the index of your nonfiction book before you read.

The index of the book also tells you what's important to the author.

Decision Time

You've previewed the book. Did you get what you needed from it? Or do you need to read it?

How Long Does It Take to Preview a Nonfiction Book?

Previewing a nonfiction book is a great way to get an overview of the book's content. This helps you decide if it's something you want to read in full. But how long does it take to preview a nonfiction book? The answer depends on what you want from the book.

Some people will say it takes between one and two hours to get a good overview of what the book is about. Take 30 minutes to preview a nonfiction book. By this time, you should have your purpose and the questions you want the book to answer. If you do what I recommended in the previous sections, there isn't a need for you to spend hours previewing.

Chapter 5

Read Only the Chapters and Sections of the Nonfiction Book That Apply to You

I 've written about how to prepare your mind to read, and how to preview a book. Now it's time to put everything together. This process is for nonfiction books. If you try it on fiction, you'll literally miss the plot. When you prepared your mind for reading, you wrote your one-sentence purpose. And you crafted the questions you wanted the book to answer.

You paid attention to the chapters and sections that aligned with your purpose and possibly answered your questions. After you previewed the book, it was decision time. Did you have enough information about what you needed from the book? Or were their sections of the nonfiction book you needed to explore more deeply?

Now it's time to read the book. Read only the chapters and sections of the book you marked as important. This is just-in-time reading. Later, you may have a different purpose, and you may need to dip into the book again. Don't worry about something that may happen in the future. And whenever you're reading a book, always tie the new information to what you already know.

As you read the book, take notes. Taking notes is learning. Therefore, it's an important part of the reading process. More than likely, you have your own way of taking notes. In the next chapter, I'll explore note-taking more deeply.

Chapter 6

Note-Taking While Reading a Nonfiction Book

T he act of reading a nonfiction book is a valuable experience for personal and professional growth. But it's also overwhelming if not approached in the right way. Effective note-taking while reading nonfiction books helps you extract the essential information and remember it for later use.

Leadership reading refers to reading with a specific purpose, focusing only on information that applies to your personal or professional goals. It requires strategic thinking and focusing on the most relevant information.

This chapter summarizes effective note-taking methods you can use while reading nonfiction books. It focuses on mind maps and the Cornell Method. If you have another way of taking notes that works well for you, continue using that method.

Mind Maps as an Effective Note-Taking Method

Mind maps are a visual representation of information. It comprises central ideas and related subtopics connected by lines or arrows. They are often used for brainstorming, organizing thoughts, and summarizing information.

Using mind maps for book notes has several advantages. It allows you to visualize the relationships between different ideas and concepts. This makes it simpler to understand the whole situation. Mind maps also keep the information organized and easily accessible.

Creating a mind map for a nonfiction book requires breaking the information into manageable pieces and creating branches for each subtopic. The central idea is placed in the center of the map, and subtopics added as branches radiating from the center.

Cornell Method for Note-Taking

The Cornell Method is a structured note-taking system that divides a sheet of paper into three sections: cue column, notes column, and summary section. In the cue column, jot down keywords or phrases. The notes' column is used to take detailed notes, and the summary section is used to summarize the information concisely.

Using the Cornell Method for book notes has several advantages. It helps you to engage with the material and promotes a deeper understanding of the information. The method also makes it easy to review the notes and remember the information for later use.

To use the Cornell Method for a nonfiction book, divide a sheet of paper into the three sections described above. While reading the book, note important information in the notes column and use the cue column to jot down keywords or phrases for quick reference.

After finishing sections or chapters that apply to you, summarize the information in the summary section.

You can buy Cornell style notebooks on Amazon. You don't have to create your own in case you were wondering.

How I Take Notes

I used to take notes in a notebook and that worked well, except I had to convert them to digital text. I record my notes using Google's recorder app, which transcribes the audio. Because I have an accent, I have to do too much cleaning up of the transcribed notes.

Now, as I read, I take notes on my computer. I turn most of my book notes into Bookish Notes for my membership site, the Art of Learning Leadership Academy. When I read the sections and chapters of a book that I flagged as important when I previewed the book, I decide what information is important and what is not.

I note the essential information. Essential information aligns with your purpose for reading the book. And also answer the questions you have, or resolve the problems you're struggling with. When taking notes, you're summarizing what you're reading.

After I finish taking notes, I let them sit for a while. Later, I will review my notes several times to re-familiarize myself with the information. I pick out the big ideas from my notes. A big idea could be any information that solves problems, cuts costs, saves time, makes processes more efficient, increases revenues and so on.

I also like to identify insights and key takeaways because these are sections of my Bookish Notes.

Chapter 7

Become a Leadership Reader - Pulling Everything Together

A leadership reader reads to learn what she needs to know. In previous chapters, you learned how to prepare your mind, preview a book, read the book, and take notes. I won't repeat that information here. This chapter is about pulling everything together.

Instead of reading a book cover-to-cover, you read only the sections that apply to your unique situation. Top leaders typically read nonfiction books because they struggle to solve a problem or they have questions to answer. So they're interested in specific types of information. The way they read is strategic and not sequential.

According to Russel Stauffer, in *Teaching Reading As a Thinking Process*, only four to 11 percent of the text on a page carries meaning. That's about one sentence of the text on an average page of a nonfiction book. So, why would you want to read a book cover-to-cover?

Here's a Francis Bacon quote that puts things into perspective.

"Some books are to be tasted, others to be swallowed, and some few to be chewed and digested; that is, some books are to be read only in parts; others to be read, but not curiously; and some few are to be read wholly, and with diligence and attention."

To become a leadership reader, there's a process for you to follow. I'll pull the steps together using a Reading Worksheet.

Set a timer for 45 minutes (You can always set the timer for another 30 minutes).

Prepare Your Mind: 5 minutes

- Name of Book

- Write your one-sentence purpose for reading the nonfiction book.

- Craft questions you want to answer.

- Do exercises to connect both sides of the brain. Choose the exercises that resonate with you.

Preview the Book: 15 minutes

- Read the preface, foreword, and introduction. Flip through the book to look at images, charts, and tables.

- View the table of contents.

- Pay attention to the index.

- Note the chapters and sections of the book that align with your purpose, answer your questions, and resolve the problem you struggle with.

Read the Book and Take Notes as You Read: 25 minutes

- Read the chapters and sections of the book you flagged as being important.

- Note the important information.

- Review your book notes a few times, picking out the big ideas, key takeaways, and insights.

- Look at your big ideas. Can you combine them to make them bigger and better? Can you tie the improved ideas to a human need?

The Reading Worksheet is only a guide. Read the Francis Bacon quote again. Treat each nonfiction book individually. Depending on how meaty the book is, you may have to allocate more time for previewing and reading.

You start off with setting the timer for 45 minutes (some people start with 30 minutes) because studies show you'll use the time you have, even if you could have completed the activity in less time. With some books, that's all the time you'll need. I set the timer for 60 minutes because I use my book notes to create my Bookish Notes for the membership site.

In another chapter, I'll introduce you to The Invisible Mentor System, so you'll get a lot more out of your reading time.

Chapter 8

PART TWO: LEADERSHIP READING IN ACTION

I t's one thing to know that leaders should be readers. But it's another thing entirely to put that knowledge into practice. In this section of the book, I'll explore the practical side of leadership reading, covering everything from reading for personal growth and development to choosing the right books.

First, I'll dive into the importance of choosing the right books. Not all books are created equal, and as a leader, your time is valuable. I'll discuss strategies for identifying the best books to read, including how to find books that align with your goals and values. And how to filter books that are of low quality or not relevant to your needs.

Next, I'll explore reading multiple books at the same time. Many successful leaders read several books concurrently, using each book to complement and enhance their understanding of the others. I'll look at strategies for balancing multiple books, staying organized, and avoiding overwhelm.

Finally, I'll discuss how to apply what you learn from your reading to your leadership practice. Reading is only valuable if you use what you learn to improve your skills and make a positive impact on your organization. I'll explore strategies for applying the insights you gain from your reading.

This includes how to share what you learn with your team, how to experiment with new ideas, and how to measure your progress. By the end of this section, you'll have a solid foundation for using reading as a tool for personal and professional growth.

they learn. And that's where most people fail. They never put what they learn into action. Besides applying what they learn, the most successful leaders behave a certain way when they gain knowledge because they're wired that way.

One thing Cunningham says that I agree with is when you are reading a book, if you come across an idea that aligns with your purpose, stop reading and apply the idea to your life. I often do that when reading. Another important point I'd love to make is that leaders aren't reading books cover-to-cover. They read strategically because they want to gain knowledge to help them achieve their goals. They read to learn what they need to know. That's the definition of leadership reading.

In the book Rich Habits, Thomas C. Corley looks at rich habits and poor habits. Rich people make ongoing learning a part of their daily life. Instead of watching TV, they study their industry by reading journals and periodicals.

"*Bad habits cause bad behavior, which results in bad decisions and ultimately a bad life. Bad thoughts occur when your mind is idle and not engaged in some constructive activity. You need to constantly be engaged in constructive activities, such as self-improvement, a worthwhile project, or a goal you want to accomplish.*" Rich Habits, Thomas C. Corley (p. 64, loc. 698)

Self-improvement activities improve your mind and expand your knowledge to better your career. As your knowledge increases, you'll notice more opportunities.

Research on the Correlation between Reading and Leadership Success

Many studies have shown a correlation between reading and leadership success. Research has found that leaders who read regularly have better critical thinking skills, make better decisions, and have a broader perspective than those who don't. A study by the University of Liverpool found that reading fiction can improve a leader's emotional intelligence. This means that a leader can be more effective at their job.

Strategies for Selecting and Prioritizing Reading Material

Leaders can select and prioritize reading material by identifying what type of information is most relevant to their current needs and goals. For example, if a leader is looking to expand their knowledge of a specific industry, they may prioritize reading books and articles on that topic. Leaders can use book recommendations from other leaders and experts, reading lists, and book reviews to discover new and interesting material.

Strategies to Read More

Reading is an integral part of leadership. The most successful leaders recognize this and dedicate time to expanding their knowledge. For top leaders to read more, they must understand why reading matters and be committed to developing a plan that works for them.

First, prioritize reading over other daily activities. Take 15–30 minutes each day to spend on something educational or inspiring. It may be a book, magazine article or even TED Talks online. This helps strengthen focus and understanding of new concepts.

Second, create short-term goals related to how much you want to read in a certain amount of time. When you have achievable goals ahead of time, it makes it easier to accomplish them because there is something tangible you're working towards.

Overcoming Barriers to Reading

Reading is essential for growth and success, yet many people face barriers that prevent them from reading. Whether it's a lack of time or access to necessary resources, individuals are hindered in their ability to read. For leaders particularly, reading presents itself as an invaluable opportunity to learn and develop the skills for successful leadership.

To help overcome these barriers, leaders must start by recognizing the importance of being a reader. Reading allows you to gain knowledge about different topics, helping to expand your mind and broaden your perspectives. It also provides you with crucial insight into how best to decide in different contexts. This kind of wisdom is invaluable in the world of leadership, because it gives leaders the confidence they need when deciding under pressure.

Chapter 10

Choosing the Right Nonfiction Books to Read

With so many nonfiction books available on the market, choosing the right ones to read can be daunting. Whether you are looking to learn more about a certain subject, expand your knowledge, or simply learn more, choosing the right nonfiction books is crucial.

I'll explore how to choose the right nonfiction books to read. You'll learn how to find books that match your interests and goals. I'll cover all aspects of nonfiction books, from the author's credibility to the quality of the content. Whether you're a seasoned reader or just starting your nonfiction reading journey, this chapter is an excellent resource for finding the right books.

Determine Your Interests and Goals for Reading a Nonfiction Book

When choosing the right nonfiction books to read, it's important to take a strategic approach. Rather than randomly selecting titles from a list or shelf, it's helpful to begin by determining your interests and goals for reading the book. Ask yourself: What subjects am I passionate about? What areas of my life or career do I want to develop further? What specific information or insights do I hope to gain from this book? Or what skills do I need to learn?

This approach helps you choose books that match your professional goals and personal interests. And it will also help you make a good investment in your time. By selecting books that resonate with your personal interests and goals, you're more likely to stay motivated and engaged throughout the reading process.

Read Reviews and Recommendations from Trusted Sources

When searching for nonfiction books to read, it's overwhelming to navigate through the countless options available. How can you determine which books are worth your time and investment? One important step is to read reviews and recommendations from trusted sources. These include well-known publications like The New York Times Book Review or Kirkus Reviews.

You can check sites like Goodreads or Book Riot. Keep in mind that reviews should not only focus on the content of the book. But also its writing style and its potential impact on readers. By reading reviews and recommendations from trusted sources, you can make an informed decision about which nonfiction book best aligns with your interests and preferences.

Research the Author's Credibility and Expertise on the Topic

When choosing a nonfiction book to read, it's important to conduct research on the author's credibility and expertise on the topic. This step is essential if you aim to gain valuable insights and knowledge from the book. Start by analyzing the author's background, credentials, and qualifications. Check if they've published any other works that relate to the topic. Or if they have any experience or education in the field.

Another way to assess the author's expertise is to look at their affiliations, such as their professional organizations or academic institutions. If the author is held in high esteem by peers or has a history of producing high-quality work in the field, this is a good sign their writing on the topic is worthy of consideration.

Be mindful of potential biases and conflicts of interests the author may have. Ensure their agenda aligns with your own interests. And that they present a balanced and well-researched argument. By doing research on the author's experience and credibility, you can make an informed decision about whether the book is worth your money and time.

Check the Publication Date and Make Sure the Information is Up-to-Date

When choosing a nonfiction book to read, it's important to ensure that the information it contains is accurate and updated. This is where checking the publication date becomes crucial. The publication date gives you an idea of how old the information is and how relevant it might be today. It's always good practice to prioritize books that have been recently published or revised.

However, not all information in older books is irrelevant. Some topics, such as history and classic literature, may still apply. And are informative even though the publication date may be decades old. It's up to your discretion to balance the age of the publication with the reliability and relevance of the information.

Look for Books that Offer Practical Advice and Solutions

When choosing nonfiction books to read, it's important to look for ones that offer practical advice and solutions. This means finding books written by experts in their field who can provide hands-on guidance on a particular topic or issue. Whether it's a personal development book or a business book, practical advice has a significant impact on your life and career.

Look for books that provide actionable steps and strategies you can apply in your life. By choosing nonfiction books with practical advice and solutions, you gain valuable knowledge and skills to improve your personal and professional life.

Consider the Writing Style and Readability of the Book

When choosing the right nonfiction book, it's important to consider the writing style and readability. It's not enough for a book to have valuable information if the writing style is dry and difficult to understand. Look for books with clear, concise writing that's easy to comprehend. A well-written book also engages you and makes the information more memorable.

Consider books that use storytelling or metaphors to explain concepts. This makes the information more relatable and helps you better understand the topic. Books with a conversational tone make the reading experience more enjoyable and help you stay engaged. When choosing a nonfiction book, make sure the writing style suits your needs and preferences and allows you to absorb the information and pages.

Preview the Table of Contents and Chapter Summaries to See if the Book Covers the Topics You're Interested In

When choosing a nonfiction book to read, previewing the table of contents and chapter summaries is a good way to find out if the book has what you need to know. Skimming through the table of contents gives you an overview of the book's entire structure.

And each section gives you a more in-depth look at the content and information. Through these previews, you can decide if the book will adequately address your areas of interest. This way, you can avoid books that may not meet your needs, and save money.

Reviewing the table of contents and chapter summaries helps you assess the book's content. This should be an important factor in your decision to read it. Taking the time to preview nonfiction books before reading them ensures you choose the right book for you and improves your reading experience.

Don't be Afraid to Put Down a Book That Isn't Engaging or Helpful and Move on to Something Else

When searching for nonfiction books to read, it's important to keep in mind that your time is valuable. Not every book is right for you. And it's important to recognize when to move on to something else. Don't be afraid to put down a book that isn't engaging or helpful, even if it's a highly recommended title. Your reading experience should be enjoyable and informative.

And sticking with a book that doesn't meet those criteria can be detrimental to your overall experience. Trust your instincts and allow yourself the freedom to search for different titles until you find one that truly resonates with you. Remember, there are many books that can give you important information. So don't force yourself through something you don't want to do.

Finding Nonfiction Books to Choose

The next step in choosing the right books to read is finding them. One technique for finding books is to search online. Online booksellers such as Amazon, Barnes & Noble, and Kobo offer a wide selection of books. They also have features that help you find the right book for you. Check online communities, where you can see what others are reading, leave reviews, and rate books. And connect with like-minded readers.

Another technique is to visit physical bookstores. Bookstores allow you to browse physical copies of books and see what's popular in different genres. Independent bookstores may offer a more curated selection of books. And you can often talk to knowledgeable staff members who can recommend books based on your interests and needs. I love browsing sections in a bookstore.

You can also ask for recommendations from friends, family, or colleagues who share your interests. They may have read books you are interested in or have suggestions based on their own reading experiences.

I subscribe to a few daily book e-zines, and I've discovered some good books. Many are off the beaten path. And the good thing is many of the books are free or heavily discounted. Another place I find the right nonfiction books to read is social media: Instagram and LinkedIn.

By incorporating these factors into your selection process, you allow yourself to expand your knowledge and perspectives. This leads to personal growth and enrichment.

Chapter 11

Reading Multiple Books on the Same Topic at Once (Syntopic Reading)

You've heard people say they read multiple books at a time. They have multiple books on the go, and they move between the books. Often the books they're reading are very different and may be a mix of fiction and nonfiction. And from different genres. That's not what this chapter is about. I'll be introducing you to a concept called syntopic reading. Before I write more about syntopic reading, it's important to focus on the benefits of reading multiple books on the same topic at once.

Benefits of Reading Multiple Books on the Same Topic at Once

Reading multiple books on the same topic provides a wealth of knowledge and insight. It allows you to gain a wider perspective of the material. You get better insights and ideas from different authors with different backgrounds. This creates new possibilities for discussion and debate. When you read multiple books on the same topic at once, it encourages you to compare different points of view. And draw your own conclusions about which theories are most valid or important.

Besides offering a wide range of perspectives, reading multiple books gives you greater depth in understanding the material. By actively looking for differences or similarities between different authors' takes on the same idea or concept, you create a unique understanding that might not have come across otherwise.

If you're like the average person, you have a to-be-read (TBR) pile of books with information that can help you. Reading more than one book at a time helps you get through your TBR pile faster. It encourages improved focus and concentration because you need to pay attention to each book separately and together. With practice, your memory improves, and you'll be able to recall more information.

Syntopic Reading

In Mortimer Adler's and Charles Van Doren's classic, How to Read a Book, they outline four levels of reading.

1. **Elementary Reading**: Level of reading that you learn in elementary school.

2. **Inspectional Reading**: Getting the most out of a book in

the time you have.

3. **Analytical Reading**: Deals with classifying the book, coming to terms with it, determining the book's message, criticizing the book and the author. Analytical reading is a very active type of reading.

4. **Syntopical Reading**: Syntopical reading or comparative reading, the most complex form of reading, is the reading of multiple books on the same subject and placing them in relation to each other.

Syntopic reading is a specific approach to reading multiple books, usually three to five, on the same topic. It involves reading multiple books simultaneously, with the goal of synthesizing information from multiple sources.

By reading multiple books in parallel, you gain a broader perspective on the subject. And you identify connections between different authors and ideas. It's an effective way to overcome the limitations of a single source. It allows you to compare and contrast different perspectives and arguments.

You can use syntopic reading if you have an urgent workplace or business problem you must solve. When you have a problem, you need diversity in thought. Therefore, it's important to read three to five books to find solutions to your problem. You spend twenty to thirty minutes on each book. It's important to use what you've learned so far about leadership reading to read books syntopically.

Simple Steps to Syntopic Reading

Choose a Topic: Select a specific topic you want to explore in depth. Think about issues you're grappling with at work. Do you have questions you want answered? Make your topic choice relevant to what's going on in your work and life.

Decide on your purpose for syntopic reading: This step ties to choosing a topic. For example, I wrote, "I'm reading books on financial health and wealth to remove money blocks and limiting beliefs, so money flows more easily into my life." My purpose helped me choose the right books.

Create a Bibliography: Compile a list of good books related to your topic. Review your list of books to find three to five that align with your purpose for syntopic reading. Continuing with my example, I chose *Happy Money: The Japanese Art of Making Peace with Your Money* by Ken Honda; *Happy Money: The Science of Happier Spending* by Elizabeth Dunn and Michael Norton; *Wired for Wealth: Change the Money Mindsets That Keep You Trapped and Unleash Your Wealth Potential* by Brad Klontz and Ted Klontz; and *Money Honey: A Simple 7-Step Guide for Getting Your Financial $hit Together* by Rachel Richards and Paula Pant.

Preview the Books: Quickly review the material to get a general sense of the content. Go to Part One of this book to scan the section on previewing books to refresh your memory. Choose different authors to get multiple perspectives and points of view. Your aim is to spend 20 to 30 minutes on each book you choose to read syntopically. Evaluate the credibility and reliability of each book. Are the authors credible?

Identify the Main Ideas: Identify the main ideas of each book. What is each book about? The main ideas are often found in the introduction section of the book. Take notes. Using a mind map to capture information from your syntopic reading makes it easy to review the information.

Compare and Contrast Information: How is the information in the books you read similar and different? Compare and contrast the different ideas and arguments presented in each book.

Identify the Gaps: Revisit your purpose for reading syntopically. Based on the information you have so far from the books, identify any gaps. Are there any inconsistencies in the information presented?

Generate New Insights: Use the information from each book to generate new insights or ideas. Are there things you discovered that were unexpected?

Synthesize the Information: Synthesize the information from all the books to create a comprehensive understanding of the topic. For example, on a blank sheet of paper, I wrote the thoughts that came to me about the four books I read syntopically. It was surprising how the information flowed easily.

Organize the Information: When I compared and contrasted the information in the books, themes emerged. Organize the information into categories or themes.

Draw Conclusions: Draw conclusions based on the synthesis of all books.

How to Choose Books for Reading on the Same Topic

Choosing books to read can be a daunting task. Especially if you're looking for something specific. Whether you want to learn about a certain topic or just to answer questions, selecting the right book is essential. Reading on the same topic is an important step in making the most of the syntopic reading experience.

But how do you know which books to pick? Here are some criteria to consider when selecting books:

Relevance: The books should be directly related to the topic you are interested in. They should cover similar content and address similar questions or themes.

Diversity of perspective: It's important to select books that offer different perspectives on the topic. This gives you a more well-rounded understanding of the subject and helps you identify common themes and ideas.

Quality: While it's important to read a variety of books, it's also important to choose books that are well-written and well-researched. Look for books that have been recommended by experts in the field or that have received positive reviews. Choose not only bestsellers. Find good books off the beaten path. There are many such books that didn't have a promotion engine to push them to bestseller status.

Accessibility: Consider the level of difficulty of the books. If you are new to the topic, it may be helpful to start with books that are more accessible and less dense.

Length of book: Consider the length of the book when deciding which one is right for you. If time is limited, opt for shorter books, so you can get through them in the time you allot.

Sources For Finding Relevant Books

Library: Public libraries are a great place to start. They offer a variety of books on different topics. And the librarians can help you find books that apply to your topic.

Online bookstores: Websites like Amazon, Barnes & Noble, and Kobo have a wide range of books available, with reviews and ratings to help you find the best books.

Recommendations from experts: Reach out to experts in the field and ask them for book recommendations. You can also ask colleagues and senior level executives.

Reviews and articles: Look for reviews and articles about books on the topic. You'll find reviews on websites such as Publishers Weekly or in academic journals. There are also many reputable bloggers who review and summarize books.

Social media: Social media platforms like Instagram, Twitter, Facebook, or LinkedIn have book clubs or groups that focus on certain topics. You can join those groups and get recommendations from the members.

Synthesizing Information from Multiple Sources

Once you have read multiple books on the same topic using the leadership reading strategy, the next step is to synthesize the information you've gathered. You can use a mind map for this. It's easy to see the information from the books visually. I prefer creating a table to see the information.

Here are some techniques for looking at the information from multiple sources:

Compare and contrast: Look for similarities and differences between the books you've read. What are the main arguments and perspectives presented by each author? What are the areas of agreement and disagreement?

Identify patterns: Look for patterns in the information you've gathered. Are there certain themes or ideas that are repeated across multiple books?

Create a summary: Summarize the main points and arguments from each book in a single document: mind map, table, or spreadsheet. This makes it easier to compare and contrast the information. It helps you identify connections and patterns that may not be immediately obvious.

Look at the Books as One

Look at your mind map, table, or spreadsheet. Soak in the information and let it incubate for a bit. Write what comes to you about the information in its entirety. You'll be surprised by what your mind notices. Never underestimate the power of your mind to make meaningful connections.

When done correctly, reading several books at the same time provides additional information that would not be possible if only one source was used. Multiple books allow readers to compare different points of view and see how different authors approach similar topics. This helps you to develop your own unique perspective based on all available data. This type of learning encourages critical thinking skills and gives readers an edge in understanding any subject.

You can use the synthesized information to support the decision-making process. And answer questions you have about the topic and solve problems.

Chapter 12

Reading for Personal Development and Growth

R eading is a valuable tool for personal development and growth. It also fosters self-awareness, critical thinking, and creativity. By now, you have a sense of leadership reading. You know how to use the reading strategy for nonfiction books. But you can also use it when reading articles and other resources.

To get the most from leadership reading, it's essential to have a goal and strategy in mind. This ensures your investment of reading time results in tangible benefits for personal development and growth. Because you're focused on what you read, you avoid wasting time on material that is not directly relevant to personal goals.

Understanding Your Goals

An overarching goal of leadership reading is personal development and growth. This encompasses a wide range of areas, including but not limited to: communication skills, decision-making, problem-solving, time management, and team management. To make the most of leadership reading, it's important to define specific areas of improvement. This helps prioritize resources and focus on areas most relevant to personal growth.

I often ask, "What is one skill that, if learned, would transform your life?"

The answer to the question above helps to focus your reading and learning, so you read only relevant books. Once you have set clear personal development goals, define the specific skills or knowledge you want to gain and what you hope to achieve, it's time to assess your current skills.

This helps you determine what you already know, what you need to learn, and where you can improve. For instance, if you want to learn a skill, chances are you already have information about the skill. Now you can identify areas for improvement. This could include areas where you need to gain more knowledge or where you can enhance your skills. By focusing on these areas, you can tailor your reading choices to best meet your personal development needs.

Choosing the Right Books and Reading Strategically

I've already covered how to choose the right books, so I won't repeat the information here. Based on your personal growth and development goals, find books to help you achieve those goals. I've also written about reading strategically, which is what leadership reading is about.

Previewing a book, reading only the relevant sections, and taking notes help to save time and maximize the effectiveness of leadership reading. This allows individuals to get a sense of the content and identify key takeaways that apply to personal development and growth.

When reading, focus on key takeaways and apply them to personal development. This includes thinking about how the information relates to individual goals, noting any areas for improvement, and talking about how to use the information to better your life.

Noting important passages and referencing them later helps to reinforce key concepts. This ensures you remember the information for future use. This serves as a valuable resource for continued personal development and growth.

Reflection and Implementation

Regularly reviewing notes and reflecting on personal growth is essential to ensure you apply the information from leadership reading. This involves evaluating the impact of the information and assessing the effectiveness of any new strategies or insights you have implemented.

Identifying new skills to develop or habits to form is an ongoing process you revisit regularly. This involves finding new resources or setting new targets to continue your personal growth and development.

Implementing new insights and strategies into your life is crucial to ensure you practice the skills you gained from leadership reading. This involves changing current routines and habits, finding new opportunities to apply new skills, and being open to feedback and change as needed.

Reading for personal development and growth is an important aspect of effective leadership reading. By setting specific goals and action plans, finding material, and regularly reviewing and reflecting on your learning and progress, you can get the most out of your leadership reading. And support your ongoing growth as a leader.

Besides the strategies mentioned above, it is also important to be open to new ideas and perspectives when reading for personal development and growth. While it's important to have a focus or area of interest, it's also important to learn about different ways to do things. By being open to new ideas and perspectives, you gain a better understanding of leadership and stay up-to-date with what is going on in the world.

Be consistent in your leadership reading and make it a regular part of your personal and professional development. By being consistent in your leadership reading, you can support your ongoing growth and development as a leader and make steady progress in your leadership development.

Be open to feedback and seek opportunities for feedback from colleagues, peers, or mentors. Feedback provides valuable insights into your strengths and areas for improvement and helps guide your focus as you continue to read and learn. By looking for feedback and being open to feedback, you support your ongoing growth and development as a leader.

Chapter 13

Using Reading to Influence Others (Becoming More Persuasive)

E ffective communication is a crucial skill for leaders who want to inspire and influence others. However, not all leaders are born with exceptional communication skills. Fortunately, reading is a powerful tool for leaders to enhance their communication abilities and influence others.

In this chapter, I'll explore the various ways in which top leaders use reading to influence others. I'll discuss the different reading leaders engage in, the benefits of reading for leaders, and how they use their reading habits to persuade, inform, and inspire others.

To help leaders incorporate reading into their leadership practices, I'll provide practical strategies. When you finish reading this chapter, you will understand how reading is a valuable tool for leaders who want to become more effective in their roles and improve their communication skills.

Types of Reading Leaders Engage In

Leaders engage in reading to enhance their knowledge and understanding of the world. Here are some of the reading that leaders often engage in:

Books: Books are a popular type of reading material for leaders. Books provide in-depth knowledge on a topic. And offers a comprehensive understanding of complex issues. Leaders often read books on various topics, including leadership, management, history, biographies, and fiction.

Articles: Articles are shorter pieces of reading material that leaders often read to keep up with the latest news and trends in their industries. Articles also provide insights into new developments and perspectives on a particular topic.

Reports: Reports are detailed documents that provide information on a specific topic. Leaders often read reports to get a better understanding of a particular issue. Or to inform their decision-making process. For example, leaders in the finance industry may read economic reports to inform their investment decisions.

Research Papers: Research papers are academic documents that present new findings or research on a particular topic. Leaders may read research papers to stay up-to-date on the latest research in their fields. Or to inform their decision-making process.

How Leaders Use Reading to Influence Others

Reading is a powerful tool for leaders to influence others. Here are ways in which leaders use reading to shape public opinion, inspire change, and persuade others:

Public Speaking: Leaders often use their reading habits to inform their public speaking engagements. By reading extensively on a topic, leaders gain an understanding of the issue and use this knowledge to craft persuasive speeches. For example, during the civil rights movement, Martin Luther King Jr. read a great deal about social justice issues in his speeches.

Writing: Leaders often write books, articles, and blogs to share their ideas and insights with others. Reading helps leaders develop their writing skills by exposing them to different writing styles and techniques. For example, former US President Barack Obama is known for his writing abilities, which he credits to his love of reading.

Interpersonal Communication: Reading also enhances a leader's interpersonal communication skills. By reading about different cultures and experiences, leaders can develop empathy and connect with others on a deeper level.

Leaders use reading to stay informed and up-to-date on the latest trends and developments in their industry or field. This helps them make informed decisions, develop new strategies, and stay ahead of their competition. For example, Warren Buffett, one of the most successful investors of all time, is known for his voracious reading habits. He has said he spends up to five hours a day reading newspapers, reports, and books to stay informed about the markets and companies he invests in.

Reading can also challenge existing beliefs and biases, which is essential for leaders who want to innovate and drive change. By reading about different perspectives and ideas, leaders broaden their horizons and develop new ways of thinking.

Chapter 14

Applying What You Learned from Reading

R eading is a valuable tool for leaders looking to improve their skills and knowledge. But it is not enough just to read. To get the most out of your reading efforts, it's important to apply what you have learned. And incorporate new ideas and concepts into your life and work. I often say that reading a book and not using the ideas is like preparing a five-course meal and not eating it.

The Importance of Applying What You Learned from Reading

Reading provides many benefits, such as increased knowledge and understanding, improved decision-making, and enhanced communication skills. However, you won't realize these benefits unless you apply what you have learned. Some benefits of applying what you learned from reading include:

Improved problem-solving skills: By applying what you learned from reading, you effectively solve problems and find creative solutions. For example, if you read a book on time management, you can use the strategies and techniques you learned to improve your productivity and manage your work.

Enhanced ability to adapt to change: Reading helps you stay informed on current events and industry trends, which helps you adapt to change. By applying what you learned, you're more responsive to changes in your industry or organization.

Improved skills: Reading helps you develop a wide range of skills, such as communication, decision-making, and problem-solving. By applying what you learned, you can effectively lead your team and drive results.

Personal growth: Reading helps you grow personally by exposing you to new ideas and ways of thinking. By applying what you learn, you expand your horizons and develop new skills and interests.

Strategies for Implementing New Ideas and Concepts into Your Life and Work

To effectively apply what you learned from reading, it's important to have a plan for implementing new ideas and concepts into your life and work. Some strategies to consider include:

Reflect on what you learned: After finishing a nonfiction book, reflect on what you learned and how it relates to you. This involves listing key points and ideas, or summarizing what you learned. Reflecting on what you read helps you remember the information and ensures you understand the material.

Identify specific actions to take: After reflecting on what you learned, identify specific actions to implement new ideas and concepts. This involves setting specific goals or creating a plan. For example, if you read a book on communication skills, set a goal to improve your public speaking skills or practice active listening with your team.

Share what you learned with others: Sharing what you learned with others helps you solidify your understanding of the material. And provides an opportunity for others to benefit from your reading. Consider sharing what you learned with your team or colleagues, or present on the topic at a company meeting.

Practice what you have learned: Implement new strategies or techniques in your work, or experiment with new ideas in a low-risk environment.

Reflect on your progress: Track your progress to ensure you're applying what you learned. It's important to reflect on your progress. This involves reviewing your goals and plan, or asking for feedback from others. By reflecting on your progress, you identify areas where you are making progress and areas where you need to improve.

Chapter 15

PART THREE: WHAT'S NEXT

Having read Leadership Reading: Spilling the Tea on How Top Leaders Read, you may be interested in exploring further ways to improve your career. I have three additional chapters to offer.

While I previously discussed effective note-taking techniques, I now want to introduce you to novel strategies that are not commonly known. If you aspire to gain expertise in a particular area and establish your personal brand, these innovative note-taking approaches will prove beneficial. With your newfound ability to select the most relevant nonfiction books to read, it is time to take your reading to the next level.

Allow me to introduce The Invisible Mentor Systems, a framework that complements your current reading habits. It enables you to discern insights others may miss, even if they read the same books. This system provides you with a unique advantage in your career development.

Chapter 16

The Invisible Mentor System to Unlock Your Genius Power

I love Rohit Bhargava's work. And I read many of the books in his Non-Obvious series he published for 10 years. Bhargava created the Haystack Method that he used to curate the trends he published in his books. I love the Haystack Method and have used it.

However, it wasn't adequate for what I wanted to do in analyzing the information in the books you read. I updated the Haystack Method and came up with The Invisible Mentor System. I'm grateful for people like Bhargava because we can stand on their shoulders and innovate.

In this chapter, you'll notice some familiar information, so I won't repeat it here. The Invisible Mentor System has two stages. You'll be familiar with several steps in Stage 1: Read Like a Leader.

Choose five books you want to read and work your way through the system using the leadership reading strategies you just learned. It's important to select a problem you'd like to solve.

Start with the first book and complete the first stage. Then read each of the other four books. When you've finished reading the five books, it's time to move to Stage 2: Leveling Up.

Stage 1: Read Like a Leader

Preparing

Before diving into the book, it's essential to prepare your mind and body to absorb the information. This includes writing your one-sentence purpose for reading a book, crafting questions you want the book to answer and doing brain gym exercises. In the Preparing Your Mind chapter, you have lots of exercises to choose from. It's also important to find a quiet and comfortable place to read and clear any distractions.

Previewing

Preview the book by scanning through the table of contents, introduction, and summary. Determine which sections need your focus and attention, and create an outline of key concepts and ideas.

Reading

Read the book with purpose and focus on specific chapters and sections that relate to your current problem or area of interest. Take notes, highlight important points, and ask questions to deepen your understanding. Review your notes and pick out and record the big ideas.

Identify and record any business model, process, or technique found in the book. You can record the information in a table. Create a table with six columns and three rows. Group the ideas to uncover a broader theme. Do you see a pattern emerging?

Testing

Apply the ideas from the book to your problem or situation. Be mindful that ideas seldom come fully formed and may require experimentation and adaptation. Did the idea solve the problem or answer your questions? If it doesn't, don't worry. What you did was a quick test. Get into the habit of testing ideas.

Repeating

Repeat the above steps for each of the other four books to gain a broad perspective on the topic and expand your knowledge. To learn a topic, you need to read at least five great books on the topic.

Stage 2: Leveling Up

Synthesizing

Draw connections among the ideas across the five books. Make ideas bigger and more encompassing. Connect models and processes across books to bridge any gaps. Identify patterns, themes, and commonalities to create a holistic understanding of the topic. What's the bigger picture? Does the idea have an underlying revenue factor? Follow the money.

Naming

Describe the newly formed ideas memorably. Use metaphors, analogies, or acronyms to make the concepts more accessible and easier to remember. Names convey meaning with simplicity. Makes it easy to share and explain.

Implementing

Test the new ideas to determine if they creatively solve your problem or improve your situation. Not all ideas are worth acting on. Take one idea and build on it. What projects are you working on where you can apply the idea? Subject it to criticism, test it, then refine it. Act and monitor the results to see if the ideas are effective.

Creating

Create something from the newly formed ideas. This could be a new product, service, process, or system that leverages the insights gained from the five books. Be creative and think differently to generate innovative solutions.

Take Your Business and Career to the Next Level

If you want to take your business and career to another level, you must act. Engage in leadership reading. Read to learn what you need to know, instead of reading sequentially. Follow The Invisible Mentor System. And make sure that you apply the ideas from the books. If you don't act, you'll never attain the level of success you desire.

Chapter 17

Next Generation of Note-Taking – Introducing You to Network Note-Taking

I've already covered mind maps and the Cornell Method. Now it's time for you to learn about network note-taking with bidirectional links. Network Note-Taking is a method of note-taking that involves creating a visual representation of the connections and relationships between different pieces of information.

It's also helpful for identifying patterns and connections that may not be immediately obvious. It allows you to see how different pieces of information relate to each other, which is useful for studying and understanding complex topics.

Digital tools like Roam Research, Obsidian, digital Zettelkasten and other services that are designed for network note-taking are great for this purpose because they make it easy to find information later on and link and organize your notes.

You can use network note-taking in combination with other note-taking methods. For example, I take notes on my computer, and then I add them to Roam Research.

Network Note-Taking with Bidirectional Links

This form of note-taking may be new to you. However, it's important that you learn how to take notes this way when reading books. Network note-taking allows you to connect your notes across the nonfiction books you read. Having this kind of access to information you learn helps you write better articles you can use to build thought leadership and develop your personal brand.

Roam Research

Roam Research is a digital note-taking tool that allows you to create interconnected notes. It allows for bidirectional linking between notes (think of those links in a Wikipedia article). This makes it easy to see connections between different pieces of information and creates a network of ideas. Roam Research also offers a variety of features such as tagging, searching, and easy navigation. It also provides easy access to notes and information, allowing you to reference relevant information.

Obsidian

Obsidian is a powerful and flexible note-taking and knowledge management tool. It uses a local folder-based system to store information and allows you to create and organize your notes in a networked manner. It's like Roam Research because it provides a space for you to organize and store your information. And it uses a graph-based structure to connect related notes.

Obsidian allows you to create and link notes in a non-linear fashion. This makes it easy to connect and cross-reference information. It provides a customizable interface. And supports a variety of plugins and integrations to enhance its functionality. Obsidian also allows you to export your notes to a variety of file formats, making it easy for you to share information with others. I have access to Obsidian, but I didn't want to have to learn another network note-taking tool. So, I haven't used it much.

One notable difference between Obsidian and Roam Research is that Obsidian is an offline application. This means all data is stored locally on your device. This provides additional privacy and security benefits. But it also means you won't have access to your notes unless you're using your device.

Digital Zettelkasten

Digital Zettelkasten is a note-taking method that originated in the 1930s. And it's based on the idea of creating a network of interconnected notes. It's been adapted to the digital age. This method of note-taking emphasizes the creation of individual notes or "slips" containing a single idea or concept. These slips are then linked to form a network of information. The goal of the Zettelkasten method is to encourage active engagement with the material and to promote a deeper understanding of the information.

Using the Zettelkasten method for book notes has several advantages. It allows individuals to create a network of interconnected ideas and information. This makes it easier to see connections and relationships between different pieces of information. The method also promotes a deeper understanding of the information and allows for easy referencing and review of the notes.

I read a book on Zettelkasten and the author used this note-taking method with Obsidian.

Other Network Note-Taking Services

I don't consider the following tools true network note-taking tools although they're classified that way.

Notion: Notion is a versatile productivity and organization tool that offers a variety of features, such as task management, calendar scheduling, and a database function. It also allows users to create interconnected notes and ideas, and to link and organize them.

Bear: A simple, easy-to-use note-taking app that allows users to create, organize and link notes, it also offers Markdown support and tagging.

Evernote: A popular note-taking app that allows users to create, organize and link notes. It also offers features such as image and audio recording, as well as web clipper.

OneNote: It's a Microsoft Windows application that allows users to create, organize and link notes and share files with other people.

These services help users create, organize, and link notes and ideas in a way that makes it easy to find and reference the information later. Each service offers a slightly different set of features and functionality. So it's important to find the one that works best for you and your needs.

How Network Note-Taking Helps You

I use Roam Research, which is a paid service. It's not the easiest platform to use. But mastering it has important implications for professionals, especially those who want to create unique content based on connected information from the books they read. To create the bidirectional links, you place the information inside double square brackets. Information includes keywords, tags, processes, techniques, or other important information.

The more you use network note-taking, the more valuable and beneficial it becomes to you. Here's an example of my Bookish Note I plan to add to Roam Research. The book is Find Your Red Thread: Make Your Big Ideas Irresistible by Tamsen Webster. The title, subtitle and author name are keywords. I've developed the habit of creating tags in my book notes when I clean them up.

Book Information

Title: [[Find Your Red Thread]]

Subtitle: [[Make Your Big Ideas Irresistible]]

Author(s): [[Tamsen Webster]]

Publication Date: May 17, 2021

Category: [[Business Communication Skills]], [[Marketing]], [[Communication Skills]]

Tags: [[big ideas]], [[red thread]]

Pages: 224

What This Means for You

If you consistently add your book notes to the Roam Research platform, it's more valuable to you. Let's say you clicked on the bidirectional link for the author's name, Tamsen Webster. You'll be taken to a page where all the names of book notes you created for that author appear. All the bidirectional links you create, when you click on them, you'll see connections and relationships with your other notes. Do you see the implication of this note-taking technology?

The Roam Research interface connects information in ways you didn't think possible. Many PhD students have said they wish Roam Research existed when they were working on their thesis. Now the owners of Roam Research have to work on making the system more user-friendly.

If you use Roam Research, the same way I use it, it's easy to learn the commands.

Chapter 18

Become an Expert Generalist and Intersection Thinker, Taking Your Career to a Higher Level

L eadership today demands a unique set of skills and capabilities. One of the key traits that distinguishes great leaders is the ability to think broadly and creatively. They connect seemingly unrelated ideas to create innovative solutions. In this chapter, we'll explore the concept of becoming an expert generalist and intersection thinker.

And examine how you can leverage these skills to enhance your career and become a more effective leader.

One trait of successful expert generalists and intersection thinkers is their willingness to experiment and embrace failure. When you are working across disciplines and exploring new ideas, inevitably, some of your ideas will fail. Rather than viewing failure as a setback, view it as an opportunity to learn and refine your approach. Embracing failure also means taking calculated risks and exploring new ideas without fear of failure.

What is an Expert Generalist?

Orit Gadiesh, Bain & Company Chairman, London, coined the term expert generalist. She defines an expert generalist as:

"Someone who has the ability and curiosity to master and collect expertise in many different disciplines, industries, skills, capabilities, countries and topics." Elon Musk is a prime example of an expert generalist, with his diverse interests and experience spanning from space travel to electric vehicles.

To become an expert generalist, you need a mindset of improving daily and a love for learning. You should seek opportunities to learn about new industries, technologies, and topics. This can be through reading books and articles, attending conferences, taking courses, and even experimenting with new hobbies.

An expert generalist doesn't just collect knowledge. They apply and monetize it. This is what I call profit reading. When you read or learn something new, ask yourself how you can apply it to your business or career. Can it solve a problem, open up a new opportunity, or help you work more efficiently?

To monetize your knowledge, you need to be creative and think differently. Look for ways to combine your expertise in different areas to create unique value.

What is Intersection Thinking?

Rohit Bhargava, author of the Non-Obvious series of books, named intersection thinking as a trend in 2019. Intersection thinking is a method for creating an overlap between disconnected ideas to generate new ideas, directions, and strategies for powering your own success. It allows you to think in a way your competitors aren't and can lead to breakthrough ideas. That's one thing you need to achieve success.

To become an intersection thinker, you need to make connections between different areas of expertise. This can be through networking with people outside your industry, reading books and articles from diverse sources, and attending conferences and events that are not directly related to your field.

Steps to Become an Expert Generalist and Intersection Thinker

Becoming an expert generalist and intersection thinker requires building a network of diverse experts. The people you surround yourself with have a profound impact on your ability to think broadly and make connections between seemingly unrelated topics. Connect with people with diverse backgrounds and expertise, and learn from them. Join industry groups, attend conferences, and find mentors who can offer guidance and expertise.

Master and collect expertise in multiple areas. This requires high curiosity and a willingness to explore new topics and ideas.

Develop a mindset to improve daily: Embrace the idea that you can always learn and grow. Cultivate a sense of curiosity about the world and seek new information and experiences.

Pursue diverse interests: Don't limit yourself to just one area of expertise. Pursue a variety of interests and hobbies, and explore different subjects and disciplines.

Find mentors: Learn from experts in different fields. Seek mentors who can share their knowledge and experience with you.

Continuously learn and develop skills: Invest in your own learning and development. Take courses, attend conferences, and read widely to expand your knowledge and skills.

Connect dots: Look for patterns and connections between different areas of knowledge. Use your broad perspective to develop new insights and ideas.

Identify and explore diverse perspectives: Look for different viewpoints and approaches to a problem or situation. Be open-minded and curious about different disciplines, cultures and ways of thinking.

Engage in cross-disciplinary collaboration: Work with individuals from different fields and industries to bring together diverse expertise and knowledge.

Look for commonalities: Identify shared concepts, principles, or themes across different disciplines. Use these commonalities to create connections and generate new ideas.

Be comfortable with ambiguity: Intersection thinking often involves dealing with uncertainty and ambiguity. Embrace the challenge of working with incomplete information or conflicting viewpoints.

Test and iterate: Generate and test ideas through experimentation and iteration. Use feedback to refine and improve your solutions.

Becoming an expert generalist and an intersection thinker requires a willingness to step outside your comfort zone and explore new areas of knowledge. It takes time, effort, and practice. But with the right mindset and approach, anyone can learn to think broadly, make connections between seemingly unrelated topics, and generate new ideas and insights.

By developing these skills, you become a more effective leader and drive innovation within your organization. The steps in this chapter provide a good place to develop these skills. But it's up to you to apply them and learn and grow during your career. Following the steps outlined in this chapter enables you to take your career to a higher level and achieve greater success and fulfillment.

Chapter 19

Conclusion

L eadership Reading: Spilling the Tea on How Top Leaders Read is a guide that offers practical strategies and techniques for maximizing your reading and personal growth potential. The book is divided into three parts that cover the ABCs of leadership reading, leadership reading in action, and what's next.

Leadership reading is an important part of ongoing leadership development. By reading strategically and using active reading strategies, you gain valuable knowledge and skills that support your personal and professional growth.

Part One of the book focused on the ABCs of leadership reading, where you learn how to prepare your mind before reading a nonfiction book, read only the sections that apply to you, take effective notes while reading, and become a leadership reader. These skills are critical for leaders who want to make the most of their reading time.

Part Two of the book focused on leadership reading in action. You learned how to choose the right nonfiction books, read multiple books on the same topic, use reading to influence others, and apply what you've learned. These skills are essential if you want to stay marketable and continuously improve your knowledge and skills.

Part Three of the book covered what's next. You learned about the Invisible Mentor System, network note-taking, and becoming an expert generalist and intersection thinker. These skills are critical for leaders who want to unlock their full potential and take their careers to the next level.

The book emphasizes the importance of reading for personal and professional growth. It shows readers how to become more effective and successful leaders by incorporating reading into their daily routine. By adopting the strategies and techniques outlined in the book, you enhance your skills, knowledge, and personal growth.

Leadership Reading: Spilling the Tea on How Top Leaders Read is an essential guide for leaders who want to make the most of their reading time. By adopting the ABCs of leadership reading, leadership reading in action, and what's next, you unlock your full potential. And take your career to the next level. Make your mark as a leadership reader.

Chapter 20

About Avil Beckford

A vil Beckford is the founder of The Invisible Mentor, The Art of Learning Leadership Academy, and The One Problem podcast. Beckford has developed an innovative program called Executive Advance: Unleash Your Genius Power, which focuses on training leaders how to read efficiently.

With this program, leaders save a significant amount of time by spending less than an hour on a nonfiction book, as opposed to the six hours or more typically required.

At The Art of Learning Leadership Academy, members gain access to Bookish Notes, which offer condensed versions of books that allow for maximum learning in minimal reading time. Beckford's expertise and vast knowledge allow members to explore a vast collection of off-the-beaten-path books, uncovering a treasure trove of wisdom and knowledge.

Chapter 21

Core Products

Unlock the power of knowledge and take your leadership and personal development skills to new heights. Become a member of the today and gain access to exclusive Bookish Notes.

(https://www.artoflearningleadershipacademy.com/)

Leadership Reading: The Executive Advantage Pro – Unlock Your Genius Power

(https://theinvisiblementor.com/product/the-executive-advantage-pro-unlock-your-genius-power/)

The 7 Day Reading Makeover Challenge to learn leadership reading strategies!

(https://theinvisiblementor.com/product/7-day-reading-makeover-challenge/)

Download your complimentary Unlock Your Genius Power Reading Tips Sheet and start reading like a leader.

(https://nameless-morning-8372.ck.page/e7990a21d7)

Subscribe to my YouTube Channel to access effective reading strategies and The One Problem podcast.

()

Chapter 22

Connect With Avil

T witter:
    LinkedIn:

Facebook:

Instagram:

Pinterest: